Your Bab

Table of Contents

Introduction

I want to thank you and congratulate you for downloading the book, Your Baby's First Year.

This book contains proven steps and strategies on how to be prepared for every stage of your infant's life. You don't want to miss a single moment because the time will pass quickly.

Here's an inescapable fact: You will need to develop a lot of patience and tolerance for to raise this bundle of joy, but you are off to a good start.

If you do not develop a roadmap of your baby's anticipated progress; you might miss an important step. The earlier you begin to chart his/her path; the happier your child can be later on when toddlerhood steps into the picture.

It's time for you to become an amazing parent during the hardest year your baby can offer; the first one!

Chapter 1: Child Development: The First Years Physical, Social, And Cognitive Development

The simplest way to understand how your precious bundle of joy will develop during his/her first year is a monthly description. Time passes quickly during the first year, and these are some of the guidelines you can gauge your child's development by during that phase:

Month One

Your baby is the most adorable human being you have ever seen. You may also notice him/her flash a look in your direction when your voice is heard. Your baby has already mastered the smell of your breast milk by the two-week marker of development.

Your hair is a favorite toy because it can be pulled, coiled, and twisted. (Mom's hair needs a ponytail for prevention.) Entertainment at this point is the silly-face game provided by Mom, Dad, Grandma, and Grandpa (or anyone else who wants to play).

> - **Body**: The tiny hands are usually clamped into little fists, and legs bunched just as he/she was in the womb. You can encourage hand opening and grasping by letting your baby grab tight on your fingers.

> - **Brain:** The baby's brain already has a head start at birth with 100 billion cells (neurons).

- ➢ **Communication Skills**: The chief communication tool is the crying trigger. It seems non-ending at this point, but before long you will recognize which cry is for what problem.

- ➢ **Senses:** At birth, things are a bit fuzzy for a newborn with vision measured as 20/400 (perfect vision is at 20/20). Your baby can see about 30 inches in any direction, so you will have to be close to be seen clearly. Your voice is recognized as well as your scent. Enjoyment at this point to your baby is hearing your voice. Talking and singing are appreciated. He/she will probably join in for a note or two.

- ➢ **Diet Plan:** Breast milk or formula is all that is essential at this point of development.

Month Two

Playtime has become the favorite part of the day with a fascination for the new mobile with its intricate shapes and movements. The 'monkey-see-monkey-do game is on the activity list as well. Imitations of your baby's sounds are excellent ways to communicate with all of the awe factors of his/her new developments. Spoiling him/her is your new favorite pass time—with your baby sound asleep on your chest for a short nap.

> **Body:** Many new physical changes are apparent including the unclenched fists, and he/she is gaining approximately one-half of a pound weekly. Neck improvement is noticeable with a wobbly movement when he/she is held upright in a sitting position.

> **Brain:** Scientists believe infants use about half of the sleepy time hours in the REM cycle where dreaming occurs. It is also a time when all of the daily input is absorbed.

> **Communication Skills:** Your youngster has begun to coo. This has the makings of a proud parent!

> **Senses:** Hugging, kissing, caressing and holding all have a unique purpose during this stage. Your touch automatically suggests an infant massage. Research has indicated mom or dad's touch can ease tummy aches, colic, and aid in immune function, as well as muscle development. The careful caresses also promote immune functions and body weight gain.

> **Diet Plan:** At this point, your nursling understands how much food it takes to eat and grow. As long as he/she

seems content, there is not any need to worry. Physicians indicate your child will eat when he/she is ready and hungry.

Month Three

You will probably notice your infant's first smile (not gas). Be prepared because it will take your breath away. Sing along at play time because your bundle of joy will love the out of tune jingle. It might be enjoyed so much you will receive a drum-roll with the new baby rattle toy that seems to be all the rage these days.

> **Body:** Yoga refers to your baby's newest improvement as the Baby Cobra. Your little one lays on his/her stomach and lifts the chest off the ground at a 45-degree angle. What a sight this is!

> **Brain:** Your baby now recognizes predictable patterns—off the main routine—including staying up later or visiting family or friends. Infants and young babies don't adapt well to changes in patterns and may become unsettled or act upset at the new challenge.

> **Communication Skills:** The time has begun with the 'a-e-i-o-u' vowel sound discovery which might sound like 'ooh and aah.'

> **Senses:** Objects are easily followed through an 180-degree arc. Eye coordination makes life more dynamic with 'patty-cake' time.

Month Four

Your little sweetheart is now beginning to giggle, and bubbles are the biggest thrill as he/she kicks back and watches them float through the air. Toys are now the scenery with a blanket or playmat. The learning process begins as you roll and inch toward your intelligent baby.

> ➤ **Body:** You will start to notice, time has rushed forward as your tyke is starting to sit with the support of his/her hands or pillow. The objects are now within reach with a bit of a stretch. What an accomplishment!

> ➤ **Brain:** Mom is the focus point because that is where the warm milk is located (breast or bottle). The sight of pleasure revolves around the nourishment. Don't worry Dad; you will get plenty of attention at the 2 a.m. feedings.

> ➤ **Communication Skills:** Your youngster is getting very smart at this point. He/she realizes all it takes is a sob or a squeal to elicit a response from you or another loving person.

> ➤ **Senses:** Colors are becoming more distinguished with the different rainbow colors coming into focus. Gone are the black and white scenery known from birth.

Month Five

Peek-a-boo is probably a favorite pass-time. The hiding of a favorite toy behind your back is a new challenge. You baby is now gaining manual dexterity and passing the toy from hand to hand.

> ➢ **Body:** Your infant's coordination is now to the point of introduction to a cup.

> ➢ **Communication Skills:** Communication is still in 'babbleville', but the conversation you provide will continue the path to encouragement.

> ➢ **Senses:** You are going to be experiencing teething soon (if not already). You may notice a skin rash, drooling, or crankiness.

> ➢ **Diet Plan:** Solid food is now on the horizon.

Month Six

You may need to begin thinking of some strategies to get your baby to sleep through the night. You are probably making the move to the big bathtub. If teeth are present, tooth brushing techniques are beginning.

> **Body:** When you support your youngster, he/she will probably be able to handle the weight on his/her legs. It might just be a crawl, but the phase is short-lived.

> **Brain:** You need to supply constant stimulation to boost motor, intellectual, and language skills.

> **Communication Skills:** The smiling, waving, and talking stage has increased, and your baby is providing entertainment to everyone who will listen.

> Beware; you might discover he/she goes exploring anywhere and everywhere for a new taste adventure— even the dog bowl.

> **Senses:** At this stage, the impulse is to touch and taste everything and anything which is in his/her path.

> **Diet Plan:** You will begin to introduce many new foods at this point. It is important to provide the new choices one at a time just in case of food allergies. Your physician will know what foods to avoid.

Month Seven

If you haven't already looked ahead on the scale of things to do' it is probably time to baby-proof the house.

- > **Body:** Your baby's focus is improving and you can tell the true color of his/her eyes by now. If there was a cross-eyed appearance before; it should be clearing out. Hand and eye coordination is improving; following the rolling ball is more intense since the colors are better focused.

- > **Brain:** Your baby's brain is running full-force and is ready to listen to the 'Itsy Bitsy Spider" and 'London Bridge' at least 1,000 times per bath.

- > **Communication Skills**: Your youngster has mastered the wave bye-bye and patty-cake stage. Don't forget the cute throwing of kisses. You might not always get the right message—so—be prepared for a few meltdowns.

- > **Senses:** The keen ears of your baby are beginning to develop while the different sounds/tones seem to be forming in his/her speech. This is the progress that develops into understanding the word 'no' in a month or so.

- > **Diet Plan:** Your baby has probably increased hunger ratings for the role of the three-meals-a-day plan. You can provide nutritional snacks but don't over-fill your hungry youngster. You will regret it when it is mealtime.

Tip: Some breastfeeding moms like to think about weaning the youngster with teeth. However, it is up to you if you are enjoying the experience.

Month Eight

You will begin to notice, by the looks of your home, that your child is mastering his/her skills nicely. It is all part of the development plan. It's only toys (hopefully).

- ➢ **Body:** This is usually the time when your growth charts are compared with other children to see if your child is appropriate for his/her age. Very few babies are overweight, but if obesity is an issue, it is best to consult with your physician. Most babies will weigh between 17.5 pounds and 22 pounds.

- ➢ **Brain:** Your active baby has many new skills, and his/her brain doesn't know which way to go first. At this age, concentration will only be focused on one toy for two or three minutes. You need to supply the learning tools.

- ➢ **Communication Skills:** Baby conversation has probably progressed to the 'ma-ma' or da-da' vocal state. If not, it will happen soon. Some parents choose this time to learn body signing as a tool to help bridge the communication gap.

- ➢ **Senses:** Your child is craving all of the input you can provide. Tastes and smells are on the scene which can provide additional challenges to you.

- ➢ **Diet Plan:** Formula or breast milk still is a good part of the baby's diet. However, you can supply 100% fruit juice (limited to four ounces or less daily). You can also provide fortified cereals, fruits, and veggies to add more vitamins and minerals to the diet of your active youngster.

Month Nine

Beware; your baby will probably decide it is time for new sleeping patterns to emerge. At least one of the daily naps will probably disappear. Playtime is much more fun; there are too many things left to do in the daytime schedule (the mind of the youngster).

> **Body:** Don't be concerned if you notice your baby's poop has changed colors. Once again, this is normal unless constipation or diarrhea is a common problem.

> **Brain:** According to research, television viewing (or other screen time activities) is not recommended for children under two years old. It can interfere with brain development in younger children.

> **Communication Skills:** Your baby might 'lose it' during this time if you try to leave him/her with a babysitter. Separation anxiety may 'kick-in' which means you need to prepare your child for the change before it occurs. Try to take your youngster to visit before you leave for work or errands. A friendly playtime or snack may all it takes to communicate the situation to your anxious/agitated child.

> **Senses:** Your child has realized how much fun it is outside by now. It is important to protect the skin with sunscreen (SPF 30) if clothing and shade aren't sufficient. He/she enjoys all of the good smells from outside.

> **Diet Plan:** A variety of baby foods should be offered along with the regular feedings of formula or breast milk. Self-feeding and a cup are probably a new part of the plan.

Month Ten

With all of the additional movement, it is essential your growing baby has all of the necessary foods needed to have a healthy start every day. So many products are on the market and with your intelligent choices; he/she will progress nicely.

> **Body:** Each activity performed reinforces his/her core muscles. He/she might topple over once in a while, but you will be there for the catch.

> **Brain:** Awareness is brought forth during this phase when you begin to ask the questions. For example, check the responses:
> 1) Where's Mommy or where's Daddy?
> 2) Find the Ball
> 3) Answer to his/her name
>
> These are all good examples of correct brain awareness of your child.

> **Communication Skills:** Speech patterns are improving, and the little genius understands terms such as, 'give me the cup please.' Mimic is a new fun event when he/she tries to make the same facial expression or echo the same sounds you provided.

> **Senses:** As time progresses, the ten-month marker can bring superb focus to your child with near and far improved vision. The hand to eye coordination is also more acute. The process is a grand one of:
> 1) Spot the toy
> 2) Focus on the toy
> 3) Move toward it
> 4) Pick it up

➢ **Diet Plan:** As your little one gets adjusted to eating, you can observe the variety and texture of the foods you serve. The pureed baby foods are nutritional, but finger foods and soft table foods are safe and fun.

What a journey!

Month Eleven

Your youngster has created more words for the dictionary, and you are there to figure out what each word means at the time it is prompted by your little chatterbox.

> **Body:** You might notice the growth pattern is slowing down a bit, and this is normal for the numbers to fly by during the first year. No child continues to grow at the rate from infancy to this point unless there is an underlying cause.

> **Brain:** Pictures in books are beginning to look really good to your kid by this time. The child-proof books can provide many hours of enjoyment for him/her, and a bit of downtime for you to collect your thoughts.

> **Communication Skills:** Skills are still progressing as your youngster figures out the difficult words. You might not get the interpretation right the first time, but you will.

> **Senses:** Your baby will realize how many textures are involved in the world; they are cold, hot, wet, dry, sticky, squishy, hard or soft. There is a unique ability emerging with the fabulous way his/her hands can grasp the bigger objects. His/her mouth might be the first choice for the item to be located, for right now.

Month Twelve

> **Body:** Your youngster can now use you for a jungle gym. After all, you are his/her favorite toy, so pulling up using you as support, is normal behavior. Put the toys on your tummy and watch the show. Your baby's weight should

have doubled or tripled from his/her birth weight and be 28 to 32 inches tall.

➢ **Brain:** Provide additional stimulation to reach his/her cognitive milestone. It's time to place a box or bag within your baby's reach of miscellaneous household objects to bang, shake, throw, or drop. Include items such as plastic funnels, winter gloves, or egg cartons. Who knows, you might have a chef in your house?

➢ **Communication Skills:** Shyness might be apparent during this time. It is important for you to be close by so you can relay the messages to the other person. Less anxiety will be given (tantrums) if you approach strangers slowly.

➢ **Senses:** Your baby realizes your touch is 'golden' because it can soothe all of the aches/pains that come along with the learning process. Introduce some objects that have moving parts so he/she can see how they all work together.

➢ **Diet Plan:** Your bundle of energy should be receiving about 1,000 calories daily. You need to provide a menu of foods that will continue to provide nutrients for good health.

Chapter 2: What Dad Can Do To Help and Support

Don't let dad believe there won't be any work for him when you and the baby come home. You will want dad's support when you come home because it will take about three weeks for your emotions to become 'un-pregnant.' You have just made a huge change in your life. It takes time and dad's patience will be needed by baby and mom.

Mom Is Over-Whelmed

Dad needs to be totally in the new picture. You need to know love and contentment are still in the scene. You feel a huge sense of responsibility, and you're not the only one experiencing this huge event; your partner is also.

Each of you can support the other partner and share the responsibilities of your new arrival. Dad; sometimes, all it takes is a few minutes to listen and be there for her. In turn, the baby can feel the love and contentment shared between loving parents.

How to Support the New Mom: The First Day Home

There are many useful ways a partner can help the new mom. These are some of those ideas:

1) Screen the visitors if necessary.
2) Keep her company.
3) Do as much cleaning and cooking as possible or organize other people to do the additional chores.

4) Provide some communication: With everything on mom's mind, it might just take a good talk to clear the air and make her day. You cannot rely on your mind reading skills. Ask what she needs.

These are all excellent tips especially when Mom and baby arrive home. The first few days will be hectic setting new patterns. Life will seem upside down for a while.

Dad's Share Breastfeeding Time

It is a known fact, dads cannot share with the breastfeeding process, but that leaves many other tasks that can be accomplished by the proud parent. Dad can still get the baby up and change the diaper. A nursing pillow and a glass of water would be an added convenience for mom. If all it takes is a bottle, (Dad) you can warm that up for Mom and baby.

Support Partner's Parenting Decisions

Support makes the job of mom and dad a simpler process when both parties can make informed decisions. Letting mom know that she is doing a great job can be all it takes to turn a blue mood into a happy event.

Be sure you (Dad) ask if it is okay you are taking over on some of the tasks. Your partner might believe she has to do all of the work. Even though she needs the help, sometimes, it is difficult to admit it.

Let Mom Sound-Off On Dad

Let her relive or talk about the labor and birth frequently if she wants to discuss the event, without becoming annoyed. Mothers usually discover it is important to repeat the huge life changing event through discussion with anyone that will listen to the continuing drama—on a daily basis.

It is not uncommon behavior for your partner to relive the event—once or a hundred times—she may continue to repeat the story more often if you ignore her. One of your important talents as a dad is to be a good listener. If you believe she is depressed, it might benefit her to seek some counseling. However, use 'kid gloves' with her because her emotions are delicate, so be prepared for a possible negative reaction.

More Feel-Good Things Dad Can Do For Mom

Meal Planning: Take over some or all of the meal planning and cooking. You can begin with a healthy breakfast as a surprise to get her day off to the right start to be sure she is eating three nutritious meals every day. She has probably been too busy with the baby to realize it was her mealtime which can often happen with young children, especially newborns.

A Massage: After giving birth, mom could probably use a nice massage. After holding the baby in her arms all day, it could be a welcomed release. You—Dad—could offer her a pleasant massage. Remember, though; Mom might not be inclined to reciprocate. You know the rules of giving and not receiving; she will let you know when it is adult playtime.

Appreciate Her: Let her know she is appreciated and buy her a personal present for no reason—just because you care. Give Mom the credit card and send her out to buy a few new clothes. Neither the clothes worn before pregnancy—nor the maternity clothes fit. New moms never have any clothes which can leave her feeling miserable without any nice, comfy clothes to wear.

It is Okay: Tell her that it is okay the home is a bit messier than usual; provide your services for a cleanup routine. Moms are usually too distracted to realize the mounting load of laundry or the sink full of baby bottles. Cleaning just isn't on the top of the 'to-do' list.

Let Mom Cry: Let Mom have a good cry or without trying to fix the problem. Lend support and a hug which can go much further during her emotional adjustment time. It is all part of the mommy blues.

Encouragement: Always provide encouragement and let her know you are proud of her and the way she is handling her new motherhood job. Frequently, let her know how much you love her, and provide praise for her great job.

Make Mom Happy: Suggest an outing (all on her own or with a friend) for a haircut/color so she can feel a bit more glamorous. Run her a bath and purchase some 'girly' magazines (something that isn't related to her new baby). Let her take over control of the remotes.

Watch Out for Mom's Emotions

Be sure your new mom has some downtime to recoup her emotions. It may seem like Mom isn't doing anything stressful, but it's a huge role to nurture a newborn baby and all of the stages involved in his/her development. Tending to a baby all day will require an unlimited amount of emotional as well as physical work.

Mom might begin to feel isolated, especially when the youngster is crying, and nothing she tries seems to be working. The result could be mom will end the process and need a tissue also. Communication for younger babies is created through the crying process which can become unnerving after a day full of the drama. It requires a lot of patience and energy for a new mom.

Try to assist and see if you can discover the problem and a cure. It could simply mean you need to settle down and cuddle with mom and baby since both are probably tuckered out by the end of the day.

Things Dads Do With the Baby

It is more to making Mom happy than just on the first few days home. It takes 100% of her time, but Dad can take many of the chores away. These are just a few of those fun events:

➤ Go for a walk with the baby so Mom can have some quiet time.

➤ Take the middle of the night feeding. The 2 a.m. bottle sometimes comes quickly to an over-tired mom.

➤ Take the early morning feeding so mom can sleep in for the day. If she is using breast milk; you can always have an extra bottle ready in the fridge.

➤ Cuddle with the crying baby if he/she won't stop crying; mom is flustered.

➤ If other children are in the home; take some of the responsibility from Mom's hands. You (Dad) can take the carpool or manage the dentist appoint for one day.

Make sure Dad knows how to change the dirty diapers and perform bath duties. Many new mothers find it enjoyable and helpful when specific jobs are set aside for Dad. It gives Mom a time to look forward to if it has been a stressful day.

Dad and the House

These are some of the things Dad can do to help around the house:

Laundry is one thing that is never done. If you notice the stack of crib sheets is depleted; maybe doing a load of them would help! Take a look around and see if the kitchen, bathroom, or lounging areas are clean.

Get Fast Food: Pick up some fast food (great comfort food) or other meals on the way home from work. You can always add some flowers (wildflowers work too) for a little 'pick-me-up for Mom.

Household Chores: Assume some of the household responsibilities such as making appointments, paying bills, or going to the market. You can always choose a store that delivers if the budget can handle the fees.

Limit Company: Make sure mom doesn't get too much company or have them 'pop-in' during inconvenient times. You can try turning off the ringer on the house phone and put the cell phones on vibrate if you are diligent and close by to intercept the calls. Be a spokesperson for the callers.

Extra Help: It isn't admitting defeat if you (Dad or Mom) decides the budget can afford a house cleaner once a week (or more). It is a lot of work with a newborn or infant in the home.

You have the point by now; if you see something that needs doing; go ahead and take the extra effort and do it without being asked. Make a conscious effort to see if any wet towels are on the floor or if the microwave needs a cleaning. It all adds up to taking the time to make the day easier for an already stressed-out mom.

It is the little things your partner will recognize, such as a shiny mirror to view the new clothes purchases. Sometimes, it is just knowing someone is there to help and mom isn't alone raising the youngster—24-7. It is a two-party job raising your little bundle, and you are the two main characters in the little bundle's life.

Additional Tips for Dad

> ➤ Try not to be solution focused on every event of the day.

> ➤ Nurture your wife by serving dinner and cleaning up after the meal at least once each week.

> ➤ It's important to be present—if needed—because you might just need to be present to listen, not work.

> ➤ Set aside some alone time for you and the baby so Mom can do some relaxing without any distractions. A nice, hot bath could be what is needed.

> ➤ Remember to include plenty of humor as you observe your newborn/infant. There will be plenty of events to laugh at—even those scrunched up looks. They are the cutest ones!

Life goes on with an infant in the house, but it is always nice when Dad remembers Mom needs the love and support too.

Chapter 3: What to Eat and What to void

Your baby will be the best guideline for your travels from infancy to his/her one-year-old birthday. You are going to learn how unpredictable your infant can become as time passes. Eventually, the skills will be mastered. After all, he/she has to start somewhere; and this is the starting point:

Four Months to Six Months: Starting Solid Foods

Your doctor will start your growing youngster with rice cereal because it is the least likely to cause any side effects. Use several tablespoons of formula or breast milk with a teaspoon of cereal. Use a soft-tipped spoon, and wait for the first reaction. Is it what you expected? You might be lucky and feed him/her a bite or two.

Begin making the cereal a bit thicker with two or three feedings daily. You should wait until he/she is approximately six months old before you introduce wheat, oats, or barley to the menu. Cereal will supplement the milk, so continue with the bottle-feedings or nursing.

It is essential to replace your child's natural iron resources from birth by the time he/she is six months old. He/she needs more than what is received from milk; via solid foods. Each time a new food is introduced, wait a minimum of three days before you add another group of goodies.

You can also discover if there are any allergies which could be indicated by rashes, diarrhea, vomiting, and persistent fussiness by introducing each food individually.

Six Months to Eight Months: Add Vegetables and Fruits

Pediatricians recommend giving your six-month-old baby veggies first since children have a tendency to prefer the sweeter foods such as fruit. It is a spoon of peas or a yummy banana; what a choice!

Yellow and orange veggies are sweeter than the green ones and can include carrots, butternut squash, or yams. Think of the holiday table. You should begin with pureed or strained vegetables and later switch over to the mashed version. You can increase the amount a few teaspoons each day (up to two tablespoons—twice daily.

Once your baby has had a few rounds of different veggies; you can they begin with some fruit. Begin with a couple of tablespoons—twice a day—avoiding sweetened treats such as puddings or cobblers.

Most babies cannot handle citrus acid in juice and others find pear and apple juices to be indigestible. It all depends on your baby and his/her unique tastes and desires.

Seven Months to Ten Months: "Bring the Lumpy Foods Please"

It is time to steer away from the 'mushy' foods your baby has been consuming. If you observe your youngster reaching for food in your plate; it's probably time for the introduction to different textures of food. The first mouthfuls of textured foods might bring a 'gag' reflex because it feels so unique.

Your tyke should be receiving 24 to 32 ounces of formula or be offered breast feedings three to five times each day. During this stage, your child will need additional sources of iron and protein, but meat doesn't always fit the taste buds of him/her at this point. Try a pureed meat with one of his/her favorite veggies (pureed beans are good) and build up to the portion to two tablespoons daily.

Special Tip: Avoid hot dogs, grapes, raisins, and nuts for your kid under five years old because they present a choking hazard.

Instead, try well-cooked pasta, cooked chopped veggies, bits of soft fruit, or toast strips—anything that has a soft texture.

Ten to Twelve Months: Dawning of "I Can Do It by Myself"

Attitude changes come along as your kid grows out of the milk-based diet. Textured and thicker foods are much simpler to prepare, such as casseroles and mashed potatoes that easily stick to a spoon. You can include finely chopped chicken, fish, or a variety of meats.

Your youngster can now have whole milk, breast milk, or soy milk from a cup. Before age two, you should introduce low-fat milk. Include two to three servings of fruit, six servings of grains, two protein foods, three vegetable servings, and three cups of milk daily.

Serving Sizes

Your child has not mastered the basic food groups, and it is time for fine-tuning the points of nutrition. Use these serving sizes as a guideline for your youngster:

> - 1 fruit/vegetable serving = ¼ cup
> - 1 grain serving = ¼ cup cereal, ½ slice bread, or 2 crackers
> - 1 protein serving = 1 ounce or ¼ cup

Other Guidelines:

> - 1 teaspoon = 1/3 Tablespoon (5 mL)
> - 1 Tablespoon = ½ ounce (15 mL)
> - 1 Cup = 8 ounces (240 mL)
> - 1 Ounce = 30 mL

As you see, his/her food groups can be included in your healthy eating plan. You can show your kid how mealtime can become another enjoyable event in his/her life of just one day.

Sample Menu for Your One-Year Old

Breakfast

- ¼ to ½ Cup Whole Milk (with or without cereal)
- 1 Cooked Egg or ½ Cup Iron-fortified breakfast cereal
  Add some Fruit either with in in the cereal:
- ½ Sliced Banana
- 2 or 3 Large Sliced Strawberries

Snack Time

- ½ Cup Whole Milk
- 1 Slice Toast or Whole Wheat Muffin
- **Add**: 1 to 2 Tablespoons Peanut Butter, Cream Cheese, or Yogurt with Cut-up Fruit

Lunch Time

- ½ Cup Whole Milk
- ½ Sandwich: Chicken, Turkey, Tuna, Egg Salad, or Peanut Butter
- ½ Cup Cooked Green Vegetables

Snack

- 1 Cup Whole Milk
- 1 to 2 Ounces String or Cubed Cheese or
  - 2 to 3 Tablespoons of Berries or Fruit

Dinner

- ½ Cup Whole Milk
- 2 to 3 Ounces Cooked Meat (Diced or Ground)
- ½ Cup Cooked Orange or Yellow Vegetables
- ½ Cup Pasta, Potato, or Rice

You can provide the same healthy choices for your entire family. There is not any need to cook for your youngster on a special plan. You might run into an objection occasionally, but continue to offer the refused foods a spoonful at a time. One day, maybe he/she will decide to like all foods.

Chapter 4: How to Breastfeed or Bottle Feed

The first choice is to decide whether you want to attempt to breastfeed or want to use the bottle. The first six months of our baby's life can be supplied by breast milk or infant formula; the choice is up to you.

Breast milk contains vitamins, minerals, enzymes, and a unique mixture of fatty acids, lactose, amino acids, and other important elements which combine to create the perfect infant diet. Everything a baby needs for brain development, healthy growth, easy digestion, and protection from illness is provided by Mom.

The American Academy of Pediatrics (AAP) states it is best for all infants to be breastfed—with rare exceptions—even sick or premature babies. Newborns will let you know when it is time to eat because he/she has already discovered where the good stuff is.

Newborns will need to nurse eight to twelve times daily, usually about ten or fifteen minutes on each breast. If crying is involved, he/she might have been hungry for a little while.

For the first six months of life, your baby has the ideal food from breast milk. If you decide breastfeeding isn't for you or decide to wean your youngster before 12 months, you should add an iron-fortified formula to his/her menu. The iron will prevent a low blood count (anemia).

Cow's milk should not be given until your child reaches the one-year marker because it doesn't have the additional vitamins needed for infants. A breastfed baby won't usually need additional water, juice, or other foods for the first six months.

How to Breastfeed

Observing a mother nursing her baby is a beautiful image with its simple and natural positions used for decades. Don't be fooled because it is not always as easy as it seems. You won't know how to play the bongo drums until you actually attempt the process. Breastfeeding also takes skill and practice. Here are the steps of survival to get the latch and hold just right for your baby:

Step 1: The Latch:

1) Begin by positioning your bundle of joy on his/her side, facing you with tummies touching.

2) Use a pillow to prop the baby's head but don't lean over his/her body.
3) Place your fingers and thumb over your areola.

4) Slightly tilt your baby's head back and use your nipple to gently tickle his/her lips.

5) Help with the process by scooping the breast into his/her mouth by placing his/her lower jaw on the nipple first.

6) While tilting the head forward, place the upper jaw firmly on the breast. Be sure at least 1 ½ inches of the areola are in his/her mouth.

Step 2: The Holds for Nursing

1) **Side-Lying**: If you want to rest while nursing your youngster—especially after a C-section—lie on the side you will be providing to him/her. Draw your baby closely to your body and place your head on a pillow. Support his/her butt with your hand while you guide your baby to the waiting breast.

2) **Cradle:** Place your baby's head in the crook of your arm and support his/her bottom with the other hand. The position should have you close with ears, shoulders, and hips in a straight line—belly to belly.

3) **Football:** You can tuck your baby on a pillow (great after a C-section) while you have him/her tucked close to your side. Rest your arm on a pillow and provide the breast while supporting the head with your hand.

Benefits of Breastfeeding

Ideally, breastfeeding should continue for at least 12 months. The World Health Organization (WHO) advises two years of breastfeeding (or more). Breast milk provides many antibodies, enzymes, anti-microbial factors, and anti-inflammatory elements with fatty acids which will promote optimal brain development.

To make the process simpler, you should sleep close to your baby.

Health Benefits

Babies can be protected from many health ailments including ear infections, bacterial meningitis, and diarrhea. It is also possible for breast milk to be a protective measure against asthma, diabetes, obesity, and sudden infant death syndrome (SIDS).

Breastfeeding is also healthy for mothers. Mom can benefit from the process because it stimulates hormones including prolactin and oxytocin which help you lose weight and bond with the baby at the same time. The risk of breast or ovarian cancer, post-menopause, as well as osteoporosis and hip fractures, are reduced.

Note: An option is also available for adoptive mothers to breastfeed. If you are one of those mothers; ask your pediatrician or your physician.

Mom's Diet While Breastfeeding

It is important to watch your diet because everything you eat; your baby is sharing the meal. Limit caffeine and alcohol. Avoid as many toxins as possible by eating organic (when possible), scrubbing your fresh fruits and vegetables, and avoiding most seafood.

About Seafood and Breastfeeding

Studies have shown many nutrients necessary for your baby's development are found in fish. The omega-3 fatty acids—DHA and EPA—are difficult to find in other food sources. You also receive vitamin D, and high protein counts, while it is low in saturated fats.

Mom, you shouldn't consume more than two fish meals each week from the non-predatory fish groups and none of the predatory fish selections. Avoid these fish:

Atlantic Cod
Atlantic Sole
Atlantic Halibut
Bluefin Tuna
Chilean Sea Bass
Grouper

Monkfish
Orange Roughy
Shark
Skate
Tilefish

Know where these are coming from:

Abalone
Anchovy
Catfish
Clams
Pacific cod
Pacific halibut
Crab
Haddock
Herring
Jellyfish
Lobster
Mackerel

Mahi-mahi
Marlin
Mullet
Octopus
Oysters
Polluck
Rockfish
Sablefish
Salmon
Sardines
Scallops
Shrimp

Snapper
Squid
Striped bass
Swordfish
Tilapia (this is one
of the most
sustainable varieties
of farmed fish)
Trout
Tuna
Whiting

The list seems overwhelming and makes you wonder what is best for your baby's health. Unfortunately, fish also contain contaminants such as mercury which can harm a baby's nervous system and brain. Mercury is everywhere, so you just need to limit the amount of fish consumed.

When in doubt, check with your physician. These are just guidelines so you understand how important it is to rear on the side of caution for your baby's health concerns.

How to Know When Your Baby is Full

It is sometimes difficult for you to know when your baby has had enough to eat. You just might not be sure if you should wake him/her up, but there is an easier way. Check for these items within 24 hours:

> ➢ Four to six wet disposable diapers or six to eight cloth diapers
> ➢ Three to four poopy diapers

These are clues your baby is getting plenty of breast milk. It is important to understand as your baby gets older the number of bowel movements (BM) will become less frequent. Don't panic around the two-month stage if your baby only does a BM once a week. It can happen.

When to Begin Solid Foods

There is no need to rush your baby's digestive track with solid foods before he/she is ready to digest them. Formula or breast milk is nutritious—besides—solid foods are sometimes just a convenience. Your baby's teeth could be a good indication—especially when one grabs the boob tightly—showing you the time is near or has arrived.

An iron-fortified rice cereal is usually introduced around the sixth month, maybe earlier. Beware of the myth; it doesn't make the baby sleep through the night. That comes using his/her own timetable!

Dark-Skinned Babies

This is a special note for you if you exclusively breastfeed your baby and offer no formula with limited solids; you need to take some extra steps. During the first year, your baby needs a vitamin D supplement or beyond if you don't receive plenty of sunshine. A lack of sun can produce weak bones (possibly rickets) during the winter months.

Dark-skinned babies are at more risk because the sunshine on their little bodies cannot withstand as much sun compared to lighter skinned babies. This is usually the result of covering your youngster when he/she is outside, especially during the winter months.

Well Water Safety

Food and formula used for consumption need to be tested for nitrate poisoning which is a risk factor for infant methemoglobinemia. The water should frequently be tested, but bottled water could be a safer choice for formula preparation.

The disease will present with a peculiar blue-gray skin color via the name of 'blue baby syndrome.' However, on the beneficial side of the coin, even if a mother drinks the water plagued with nitrates, a breastfed baby won't be at risk.

When in Doubt

The Centers for Disease Control and Prevention (CDC) has indicated three out of four mothers in the United States will breastfeed her baby because it is a natural process. If you need additional support for breastfeeding, you can ask your physician or check online for additional information from the National Association of Pediatric Nurse Practitioners.

How to Bottle Feed

Providing the correct formula can be a matter of trial and error, but you should choose one that is iron-fortified. It shouldn't be necessary to use a low-iron formula unless there is a family history of allergies or believe he/she could be lactose intolerant. You can choose from ready-to-feed forms (convenient but more expensive), or one in a concentrated powder form which will be mixed with water.

You can use the cradle position (previously described) in a semi-upright position, but never feed him/her lying down. The formula can flow into the child's inner and cause an infection. Tilt the bottle, so the formula fills the bottle's neck and covers the nipple to prevent him/her from sucking air while drinking.

For the first few weeks, you can expect the child to consume between two to four ounces for each feeding. (It may be less than an ounce for the first few days of adjustment.) As a guideline, expect to provide feedings every two to four hours, but your baby will make his/her own timetable.

Don't try to force-feed your youngster. He/she will let you know when enough is enough. If he/she is still contently sucking away; you can offer more.

The Burping Process

Burping is the process used to prevent too much air from remaining in the baby's tummy. The fussing can become a vicious circle, creating more air into an already unhappy youngster. Try to burp him/her after every two or three ounces of formula. After a couple of minutes of the burping stage, resume the feeding. These are three great positions to try:

1) **On the Lap**: Sit your baby upright and lean the weight forward against the heel of your hand as you firmly rub or pat his/her back.

2) **Lying Down:** Place your baby, stomach-down, on your lap while you firmly pat or rub his/her back.

3) **Over the Shoulder**: Lift your baby over your shoulder and firmly rub or pat his/her back.

Chapter 5: How to Bathe Your Baby

Bathing your newborn baby is an exciting event, for Mom and Dad! The youngster is probably still considering going back into the womb where it looked a lot safer. These are a few of the steps to guide you through the bathing experience from newborn until he/she is one-year-old.

Newborn Bath Time

It isn't necessary to give a full bath to your newborn because it can tend to dry out the skin. If you are speedy with the burp cloths and clean diapers, you have already cleaned the parts that need the most attention.

For approximately the first week; it will be best to provide a sponge bath using a warm—damp washcloth (just his/her size). Provide frequent touchups to that cute little face and don't forget those hands. Be sure to thoroughly clean the diaper area after each change to eliminate additional bacteria.

Baby Tub Time

After the umbilical cord stump falls off and heals; every few days your newborn can receive a tub bath. Many people use the kitchen sink or a small plastic baby tub versus the standard adult tub.

During the newborn stage, he/she is not busy crawling everywhere and getting into everything, so more than three baths weekly during the first year is fine. Depending on your child's reaction to the water, a five-minute bath should be sufficient to clean all of the important parts.

Don't worry; you will get over the scary situations of handling a wet, soapy, and wiggling baby. It takes practice, just hang on, stay calm, and it will go smoothly.

Time It is Best To Bathe

Choose a time that is most convenient when you don't have to rush or be interrupted. Some parents enjoy the solitude of a morning bath to wash away the diaper smells from the night before. Others believe the bedtime ritual is a better time. You are the leader, so experiment and see which way works best for your baby.

How to Give a Sponge-Bath

Before you begin, gather all of the supplies you will need to ensure you won't need to leave your baby unattended.

1) **Choose a flat surface in a warm spot**. Warmth is the most essential element. You can choose a towel on the floor, the changing table, bathroom or kitchen counter, or even the bed will be okay.

2) **Provide a soft towel, blanket, or changing pad**. Spread out the item for the baby.

3) **Use your free/empty hand**. Always have one hand on the baby. If you are using a changing table, be sure to use the safety strap for additional protection.

4) **Place some water in a shallow basin or sink**. Check to be sure the water is not too hot.

5) **Undress the baby and place him/her in a towel**. Place your baby on his/her back on the towel.

6) **Wet the cloth and wring out any excess water**. (No need for soap).

7) **Use a clean cloth or cotton ball to clean each eyelid**. Wipe from the inside to the outside corner.

8) **Be sure your baby is completely dry and dress**.

Safety First

Never—even one-minute—leave your baby in any water unsupervised. If the doorbell or phone persists on ringing; grab a towel and the baby to proceed. The brutal fact is a child can drown in 60-seconds in less than an inch of water.

Set the water heater temperature to 120 degrees Fahrenheit; third-degree burns can happen in 140 degrees in less than a minute. The bath water should remain around 100 degrees Fahrenheit, so the baby doesn't become chilled.

Wait until the after the water has stopped running to ensure it isn't too hot or too deep. The amount of water used is debatable at best. The Mayo Clinic suggests two to three inches is recommended which is about five to eight centimeters. Whereas, others suggest enough water to cover the baby's shoulders can be used.

Steps for A Safe Tub Bath Experience

Step 1: Gather or lay out all of the necessary supplies (shown below). Be sure the room is warm for the baby's bath time.

Step 2: Fill the tub with warm water (no more than 3 inches). Test the water as you would a baby bottle—on the inside of your wrist. The water should be between 90 and 100 degrees Fahrenheit.

Step 3: Undress you baby in the bath area. (If your baby dislikes the water, try to leave the diaper on at first). Some believe this helps with security issues the child might have from the water.

Step 4: Gently place your baby in the water (feet first) while the other hand supports the neck and head. During the bath, pour some warm water over his/her head, so he/she doesn't become chilled

Step 5: Begin with the baby's scalp with baby shampoo/body wash with a small amount of soap on a washcloth. Remove the soap from the rag and gently wipe his/her face. Work your way to his/her bottom.

Step 6: Rinse your sweetheart thoroughly with cups of water, and wipe with a clean washcloth.

Step 7: Carefully, lift him/her from the tub with one hand on his/her butt and the other supporting the neck and head. If Dad is around; ask for some assistance.

Step 8: Wrap your little bundle in a hooded or regular towel and pat his/her body from head to toe. If you see some dry skin, use some baby lotion to relieve the affected areas. It could be just a layer of dead skin which will come off in good time.

Step 9: The process is complete except for the diaper, dressing, and kissing the sweet angel you just cleaned.

Supplies Needed

> ➢ Mild soap
> ➢ A washcloth or two
> ➢ Plastic cup (to help remove the soap)
> ➢ A Diaper
> ➢ A towel (regular or hooded for baby)
> ➢ Clothes

Chapter 6: The Sleeping Routine

Your child's journey with unique behavior begins at newborn. He/she might depend on you entirely, but they surely don't take your cues when it comes to sleeping and eating. A routine is usually in place by the sixth month, but until then—be prepared for some sleepless nights. His/her age, feeding hours, and physical activities will be the major factors used to determine the sleeping schedules.

Newborn to One Month: At this stage, your baby will sleep the majority of the day and be awake long enough to be fed. Kids can usually sleep fifteen hours out of the twenty-four because his/her biological clock isn't programmed.

One Month to Four Months: Most babies will have a set routine of waking times and sleepy times. You will begin to notice the predictable patterns.

Four Months to Twelve Months: After the six-month marker, the sleeping pattern shrinks from sixteen hours to twelve hours. The increased mental and physical changes will also have an effect on his/her naptime. Mid-morning to early evening naps is the most common times for a snooze. This chart will make the markers clearer:

Months by Age	Total Sleep	Daytime Sleep	Bedtime Sleep
Newborn to 2 months	16 to 18 hours	8 to 9 hours	3 to 5 naps (up to 9 hours)
2 to 4 months	14 to 16 hours	9 to 10 hours	3 naps (up to 5 hours)
4 to 6 months	14 to 15 hours	10 hours	2 to 3 naps (4 to 5 hours)
6 to 9 months	14 hours	10 to 11 hours	2 naps (3 to 4 hours)
9 to 12 months	14 hours	10 to 12 hours	2 naps (up to 3 hours)

Establish the Sleeping Schedule

Specific guidelines will help you create what is normal for our child. These are some of the hints to help you through the process:

Step 1: Be sure your baby is tired. If your youngster is still energetic and ready to go, you will not get him or her to sleep. You need to wait for signs of tired behavior such as yawning or droopy eyelids.

Step 2: Set the sleep cycle: Get your baby tuned in with daylight hours by creating activities (depending on the age group). Decrease the activity and participation levels during nighttime activities. Dim the lights and turn down the noise levels. Remove any stimulating or noisy toys to eliminate the motion factor. Baby mobiles can help with the 'outside of the crib' distraction.

Step 3: Separate sleeping and feeding schedules: Most children will go to sleep soon after a meal. The secret is keeping him/her awake until he/she has been completely fed. Don't force the eating habits because you can cause an outburst of moods. It is beneficial to let your child learn how to sleep on his/her own.

Step 4: Don't wake the baby for a feeding. After two months old; you can let your baby sleep through the nighttime feeding routine. Your baby should develop his/her own eating patterns, but you should monitor the pattern. If your baby is under two months old, you shouldn't allow him/her to sleep without eating for more than four hours at a time.

Step 4: Set a routine early in life: You pave the way for a functional daytime routine if your youngster has a set bedtime routine. You can begin a plan after the first two months, but try to keep them simple. Start with a bath, a feeding, and lights out. Of course, your infant might enjoy a lullaby for the first few weeks, but after that let him/her figure the rest out solo.

Step 5: Adapt the schedule according to his/her age. Be reasonable and stay close to a pattern. Of course, it isn't yet set in stone. You have the reins, but he/she will lead the way.

Nighttime Wake-Up Calls

Many studies have been provided to discover the attachment to parents and waking up in the middle of the night. Much of the data is varied by age groups and situations; however, 50% of the infants (even the 12-month old group), required intervention by the parent to get back to sleep.

Patterns of a Six Month Old

Sleep research has indicated through the parents of 640 babies, of what is normal for a six-month-old tyke. The following:

- ➤ 84% were not sleeping through the night—16% slept through the night at the same age.
- ➤ 50% woke occasionally
- ➤ 17% woke more than once (2 to 8 times)
- ➤ 16% had no regular sleeping pattern
- ➤ 9% woke most nights
- ➤ 5% woke once every night

Further research was provided by mothers of 118 infants of sleeping patterns of their children from 3, 6, 9, and 12 months. As you see; it is a common characteristic for your baby to require your attention in the middle of the night. This is an average of the results:

Baby's Age	Babies Waking Up At Night
3 Months	46%
6 Months	39%
9 Months	58%
12 Months	55%

The increase of night walking events toward the end of the first year coincides with characteristic socio-emotional advances during this stage of development.

Chapter 7: What To Do With a Sick Baby

As a parent, you are the first to know when it is time for some special medical care. It is all in a process you will figure out as you go down the road to toddlerhood. These are some of the situations you may be faced with during your baby's first year:

Medical Issues

Dehydration: When you have a sick youngster, one of the biggest triggers for illness is dehydration. Children younger than six months old usually become dehydrated quicker than older children. Children under one-year-old need about one quart of fluid daily; depending on your baby's size. The amount needed increases as the body fluid is lost. A fever causes fluid to seep through the skin, creating the field for dehydration.

You will notice dryness of the tongue, mouth, and lips. In severe instances, the child can lose the mechanism for thirst and not want any fluids. Dark circles under the eyes and dry skin may appear after a few days. Since your baby is under one-year-old, you might notice the soft spot (the fontanel) may appear flatter than usual or sunken.

A weak but rapid pulse or rapid breathing could also be a sign of severe dehydration. He/she might be unaware of the activity in his/her general area (a huge warning sign). If you notice the skin looking doughy or wrinkled as well as the dry lips, you should call 911.

> ➢ **Note:** Breastfed babies can continue with the breast milk diet but should be fed more than normal (at least every

one to two hours) or smaller amounts for five to ten minutes at a time. You can pump and provide portions of milk by bottle, spoon, or cup; any way you can get him/her to drink the liquids.

Infants who are drinking formula can continue drinking the full-strength regular formula.

The Fever: Usually, an underlying problem is indicated when fever is indicated. The body temperature rises because infection-fighting enzymes fight infection best at high temperatures. A fever can be the in relation to a cold, the flu, an ear infection, or a reaction to a recent vaccine. Your baby might be a bit irritable and lethargic. Try serving a regular diet, but add some favorite sauces to increase each bite of the caloric content. Push the fluids.

A temperature of 101 degrees or below isn't usually a trigger for danger. Try to cool the baby down in tepid bath water, and encourage him/her to drink fluids. It is advisable to provide Infants' Tylenol.

For a newborn (2 months or younger), you should call the doctor even for a low-grade fever. If your child is younger than one-year-old with a fever of 102, you should make the call.

The Common Cold: Children can average getting a cold at least six to eight times each year. You will notice coughing, sneezing, a runny nose, and maybe a fever. It will usually build up for two to three days, and peak around three to five days before it subsides.

It is beneficial to run a humidifier in the baby's room while he/she is sleeping if your infant is congested. Try elevating the bed with books or pillows under the mattress.

If there is no interest in formula or breast milk, try giving him/her water or Pedialyte (or any electrolyte drink). Offer some warm, comforting foods such as chicken soup. Try to find some with the cute characters or letters for some conversation pieces.

Call the doctor if your newborn is sniffling or has a high fever (as described above).

Coughing: While the cough is present, offer small amounts of clear, warm fluids to help remove/thin-out mucus for older babies. Try one to three teaspoons of warm water or apple juice as a remedy.

> **Urgent Tip**: Don't offer honey to a child younger than 12 months old. Infant botulism is an illness that can be contracted if the baby ingests bacteria that produces the toxin inside his/her body. The American Academy of Pediatrics (AAP) and The World Health Organization (WHO) also state honey should not be added to formula, water, or any food prepared for infants younger than 12 months old. For more information, it is best to ask your doctor.

Ear Infections: Many babies, especially newborns, and infants, rub the ears. You need to pay attention to the other body languages which are displayed such as the stuffy nose and ear infection if it is grouped with the tugging of his/her ears. Some infections will pass, but others may need antibiotics. Once again Infants' Tylenol will help the baby sleep.

If the symptoms don't improve in a few days, you will need to visit the doctor. The issue could become severe enough to infections which could lead to repeated ear infections, hearing loss, or a ruptured eardrum.

Respiratory Syncytial Virus (RSV): Preemies are extremely vulnerable to this common virus that has an effect on the lungs and breathing passages because his/her lungs are under-developed.

The symptoms are similar to the common cold, but by the third day, a strong wheezy-like breathing and cough begin. A cough could linger for as long as two weeks. The other symptoms should be gone after several days. A bad episode can develop into asthma.

If you have a sick newborn, don't hesitate to call your doctor. Observe closely to see if he/she is breathing normally. Take off the baby's shirt and check the spaces between the ribs. If the spaces are sucked in with his/her breath, and the nostrils are flaring; call a rescue team immediately.

Gastro-esophageal Reflux (GER): The first few months bring varying degrees of GER which can cause pain when the acidic stomach contents regurgitate into the esophagus. The issue is sometimes diagnosed as colic (sometimes called the hurting baby). You may notice your baby throwing the legs up or arching the back as well as frequent vomiting/spitting up.

You might need to attempt smaller, more frequent feedings. As a result, the reflux should calm down, and allow more production of saliva which also helps reduce the stomach acid.

Constipation: Try serving your child some prune juice or prunes to get things going again. High-fiber foods are good sources for constipation relief, such as oranges, carrots, celery, and apples (if he/she is ready for them), as well as water, will help keep stools more regular.

Conjunctivitis or Pinkeye: You will notice your baby's eyes look red and puffy because of the inflammation of the eye's mucous membranes. It can be in one or both eyes. The condition can be caused by either a viral or bacterial infection, and be accompanied by green drainage signals (bacterial) or pus with no tearing (viral). Either form is highly contagious and will quickly spread to others.

You will need to keep the baby's eyes clean by gently washing them warm water. The problem will probably subside within a week. Antibiotics will be given if it is a bacterial infection. You can make your sick baby's eyes feel better with a warm compress. Don't share the washrags or towels.

Diarrhea: Several reasons could be why you are changing such nasty diapers:

1) **Virus**: These are usually frequent and runny.
2) **Bacterial**: This could be caused by food intolerance, allergies, or medicines.

Diarrhea will usually run its course from five to ten days, but dehydration is the main concern. If he/she is also vomiting; wait 30 minutes after he/she has thrown up and offer frequent, small doses of an electrolyte drink. You should begin with a tablespoon as a guideline and increase the amount over time.

Avoid juice and soft drinks because sugar can worsen diarrhea. Try some binding foods such as cooked veggies, ripe bananas, or rice.

If you notice bloody diarrhea or a high fever, you should call the doctor.

Stuffy Nose

You can use over-the-counter saline spray, gel, or drops to thin the mucous around your baby's nose. Your doctor can advise which product best suits your child's needs. Generally two drops in each nostril will cure the problem.

You can also use a nasal syringe to remove the nose of mucus so he/she can breathe easier. You can clear the nasal passages two or three times each day.

Congestion can be relieved with a cold-mist humidifier in your infant's room. (Warm-mist spray has a danger of scalding). Follow all of the manufacturer's recommendations and clean the unit regularly. Use fresh/clean water with each daily use to prevent bacteria or mold buildup.

How to Give Medication

Caution must be taken when you provide your baby with medication. Children are more sensitive to medications versus adults. Before you give any medication to your child, be sure you have received the complete instructions from your doctor and pharmacist. You need to know of any side effects could occur and how long the medication should be given to your child.

You also need to know whether it is to be taken with or without food. Some medicines work best on a full tummy whereas others work best when nothing has been eaten.

Most pharmacies clearly label each product sold, but it cannot hurt to know all of the facts. You are the responsible caregiver who is responsible for your bundle of joy and his/her health. You must understand the pros and cons before you begin the regimen.

If you are using over-the-counter medicines; be sure to carefully read the charts for the correct dosage—size, weight, and age specifications.

Tips on the Right Dose

These are just a few of the items that might be tricky on medicine delivery to your infant:

> Be sure of your baby's weight. Many of the doses are based on weight, but some are on age and weight. If you are unsure, use the weight from the child's last doctor visit. You could always hold the child in your arms on a bathroom scale, and subtract your weight to discover a more accurate weight for the medication.

> Some of the over-the-counter medications for babies are concentrated (Be sure not to give a child a normal dose).

> If a label says to shake; by all means, do shake it. It is to ensure your baby is receiving all of the ingredients and not receive the wrong distribution of any of its parts.

> Don't confuse tablespoons (T or Tbsp.) with teaspoons (t or tsp.). Not many baby medications will require a tablespoon as a rule-of-thumb.

The best medicine for your sick baby is a lot of TLC. Hold the little hand and provide an infant massage to work out the pains. If you are breastfeeding, he/she might want to nurse more—for reassurance—as much as anything else. Your soothing voice is a huge part of what will make him/her feel safer.

How to Give the TLC

> ➢ Provide a cuddle and a back rub until the medicine takes effect.

> ➢ Try the steam from a hot shower. (Run the water as hot as possible and sit in the room with your baby).

> ➢ Provide endless singing and rocking. Modify the words for a bit of personal humor after about the tenth version.

> ➢ Provide a tepid bath to help with the aches and congestion.

You will know what works best after a few trial runs. You just need to keep improving. Your baby knows you are the one that will fix it all.

Be Prepared for Emergencies

An old motto of being prepared best suits the situation when your baby is sick and you might also be sick. Here are a few ways to be prepared for the next unexpected illness:

Stash New Toys: It's a known fact that most babies (especially the first year) have more than he/she can possibly play with at once during Christmas or birthday parties. After you discover if he/she likes the toy; stash it away for the sick day.

Pre-stock Bland Foods: It is always best to have a supply of rice cereal, applesauce, saltines, and maybe a banana or so for the day your baby has a tummy bug. Be sure to stock enough for you too since you are with him/her closely, you might also get sick.

Locate a Pharmacy Delivery Service: Set up a house account so if you need a special prescription, you can get it and not need to leave your sick kid.

Pamper Yourself

Yes; this sounds a bit out of place, but how is your baby going to receive quality sick care if Mom is not feeling desirable?

Accept the Extra Help: You have heard the story of, " I will do anything, just let me know," before right? Take him/her up on the offer and run some alone-time errands. It will make you feel better to just leave the house for a few minutes.

If no one has volunteered, search for someone to come in and help with some of the housework. If the budget allows, hire a babysitter and go out to dinner with your partner.

Stay Healthy: Take a walk and take in some sunshine (vitamin D) or go into another room and do a series of jumping jacks. If you just don't have time, at least take some multi-vitamins and calcium to stay in shape. You cannot take care of a sick baby if you get sick!

Splurge on Caffeine: If you aren't breastfeeding; take a break with some caffeine and go have a yummy treat at the café up the street. Just get a boost.

Take a Nap: You probably think a nap is selfish because—after all—you're Super Mom. There is nothing wrong with a power nap while your sick youngster is napping. You will be there if he/she needs you; just more refreshed.

Chapter 8: Communication Techniques

Understanding your baby takes many hours of love, concentration, and patience—but—it is so worth it. Babies are born with the natural ability to cry. As a parent, you have to choose ways to discover the reason for the problem whether it is cold feet, a wet bottom, or hundreds of other problems.

Your little bundle communicates with you through touch, warmth, food and all of his/her care.

The first year of communication begins with smiles, gurgles, and coos and the many babbles right back. Smile back often so he/she knows the thought is getting to you. Keep a close watch as he/she laughs and tells you another baby secret. Never look away or interrupt by talking to someone else.

Be patient as you begin to decipher what is being relayed through those cute facial expressions—happiness or sadness—will be revealed.

The Baby Voice

Many people believe it isn't proper to talk in the special tone of voice when speaking to a baby. Physicians believe the natural baby talk mimics the female voice which in turn relates to the baby as dinner/feeding time or comfort. It naturally brings a huge smile. On the other hand, it also is believed to have nothing to do with speech development later on in the baby's life. So coo away!

He/she cannot communicate as intently during the newborn stage, but with patience and guidance you will discover many useful tools. These are a few ways to help with your child's development:

How to Promote Communication and Language Skills

Practice	Description
Be Talkative	Exchange in conversation with your child
Be the Anchorperson or Announcer	Provide descriptions of events, activities, and objects
Mix Everything Up: Change the Patterns	Different words and grammar are passed around
Put a Label on It	Provide kids with names of actions and objects
Interactive Reading Skills Required	Use Books to get the kid's attention
Get Tuned In	Engage in objects and activities that are of interest to your baby.
Read it Again—Again—Again	Reading the same books— over—and—over.
Make Some Music	Musical activity engagements
Where are the Props?	Introduce conversation pieces (objects) to the baby
Sign It Please	Use simple signs with words or use gestures

Step 1: Be Talkative: The more words you child hears, the more ways he/she can receive the 'input' needed to form a vocabulary. Children love it when you use your hands. The more

opportunities you provide for the input—the better the understanding and comprehension of your child.

Step 2: Be the Anchor: Make it a point of conversation about the right way to wash his/her hands or how the best way is to hold a spoon. Make a model language by commenting on events such as the bird in the yard or the dog barking. Make him/her associate the new sounds with you as the anchor point.

Step 3: Mix It Up: Use your robot voice and say something like, 'I have a new ball under the table.' Repeat the words another way such as, 'Do you want the new ball under the table? Make him or her think about what you said.

Step 4: Label It: Now; you have your baby's attention—continue from step 3. 'I have a new blue ball under the table.' 'Do you want the new blue ball under the table? You gave the item a name (more input). Point at the ball and repeat the information. Repeat the words often.

Step 5: Interactive Reading: It is time to relocate your animated voice again. Locate a baby-proof book if your baby has mastered the pinch and grab stage. Point and place a label on each action in the book. Make squeaky or banging noises for the older tykes or a gentle voice for infants. Your baby will let you know if you are doing it right!

Step 6: Tune In: You need to pay close attention to see what your baby is focused on at the moment. It is up to you to ask all of the right questions of what, why, and how. Give the focused item a name and you will be totally tuned into your baby's channel of thoughts.

Step: 7: Read It: You know you have done a great job in communication when your youngster either squeals—again—again—or starts to pat the book. The reaction will, of course, depend on the baby's age group.

Step 8: Bring the Music: It is time to bring 'The Wheels on the Bus' and all of the simple songs of youth. If your youngster is attempting the words—slow down—let him/her have the stage.

Step 9: Bring the Props: You have the rhythm; now you need to locate some photos of family and friends or some puppets. Have a puppet show provide a few new words or behavior themes (good versus bad).

Step 10: Sign It! Each baby is different but why not provide a few more advantages and teach him/her sign language. Babies are very receptive to new information. Say simple words like cup or milk and use the sign for the word. Make the child believe it is a new game, not a learning tool. Repetition is the key to learning.

The One-Year Stage of Chatter

By this time, your baby has begun to understand more words than he/she can pronounce. Using gestures is an important skill to encourage, but you also want to encourage, the use of real words. After all, you don't want your baby to always call the bottle a "ba-ba." Use your regular tone of voice and watch as the vocabulary increases.

Sit down for some quiet time with a book during times of the day when he/she isn't tired or sleepy. It is a lot more fun to practice speaking skills when your baby isn't about to rub the eyes out of the socket! Talk about what is happening in each picture—and ask questions. You might not understand the response, but you will probably hear one.

Plan Play Dates

It is important to socialize your child with other kids in his/her age group. It gives him/her time to interact and listen to other children. Testing the vocabulary you have provided might be entertaining to observe with others. You can always add in a 'please' and 'thank-you' for the group.

> **Up to Six Months:** Okay, so at this point a play date is really more fun for mom or dad. You have probably been in the house with the baby for the past week or month and just need some grown-up conversation. Locate parents of children who are the same age as your child. It will be fun to compare doctors, swap stories, and chat about everything.

> **Six Months to One Year**: The game becomes two-way by now, and you and your kid are enjoying play dates. Everyone is on the floor crawling around, and to your child, you probably look silly. It makes the game more fun. You are teaching your child good social skills. Interaction cannot begin too early in your child's life.

Chapter 9: How to Exercise and Play with Your Baby

Increase your baby's head control and neck strength:

Head Rotation: Ages of Infancy to two-month-olds should now be able to lift his/her head and turn side to side. You need to encourage equal movement on both sides. Use a bright colored toy or a moving light toy to catch his/her focus. Move the object slowly to encourage the focus.

Use crib toys are on the 'unfavored side' so the baby will need to be more determined to view them. You are already entertainment on the other side of the crib.

Tummy Time Activities: You can begin the skin-to-skin method with newborns with the baby lying on your stomach. You can alter the position for comfort. He/she has already learned for at least nine months of how comforting Mom's heartbeat is at all times.

Neck Flexion with Pull to Sitting Position: By the time your baby is six months old, he/she will not have a head lag with the pull to sitting movement. Your baby should be able to lift the head and bring his/her chin forward—sitting—or—on the back. You can begin with the baby propped up in a sitting position until his/her neck strength is improved. Be close in case his/her head decides to take an unexpected turn or drop.

Older Version of Tummy Time

Once your baby has mastered holding his/her head upright without a struggle, you will discover placing his/her weight on your hip helps with your 'back' issues. During the process, rotate hips frequently to encourage head movement from your passenger.

Tummy time is an important tool which aids your baby to roll over, crawl, and eventually walk. You may also notice little muscle development in his/her neck, arms, shoulders, and upper back.

> ➢ Workout one involves laying your precious bundle on his/her tummy on the floor. Use different colors and textures as you continue to improve the presentation of 'hold your head up baby.'

> ➢ Help the process by carrying your baby facing away from you, so he/she can see the world from your perspective.

> ➢ Make a play date with a friend because socialization cannot begin too early.

> ➢ Set aside 15 to 20 minutes of activity daily, or five-minute intervals three times a day to get a routine in place.

It is important to continue with your tummy time program to ensure your baby will learn to walk properly. His/her muscles are still under development and need some extra guidance from you. Try holding or carrying your baby belly-down while supporting his/her chest and head.

Recommended Games

Each phase of development requires a different trigger to keep your baby properly entertained and on target with each phase. These are the different stages of imagination:

Newborn

Fingers and Toes: Who needs toys from the newborn stage to three months (maybe beyond) with the new touch sensitivity provided by his/her own feet? You can enhance the experience by showing him/her how easily the hands open up as you gently rub his/her hands and fingers. The amazement of human body parts from the baby's perspective.

Gentle Rubdown Time: This sensational method is a prize-winner for newborns up to the age of ten months. Touch and sensitivity are created as the touch of a furry animal or a soft baby blanket draped over his/her body. Start a collection of different textures for your baby's enjoyment and developmental skills.

Happy Talk: Begin preparation for speech with nothing but your voice and imagination for your newborn until around the four-month line. Start out by making the gentle 'ahh' sound by showing him/her how to make the noise using his mouth. Keep repeating the sound.

You can also make an exaggerated kiss back at your cuddly youngster. The association will begin to click in his/her head.

Two Months Old

The Dilemma of Sound: Babies have a natural inclination to become startled by loud noises. With your reassurance, he/she will learn many other interesting noises such as rattling and squeaking sounds. You provide the connection.

From two until about five months, it's a great time to provide some 'cause and effect' choices for your baby's enjoyment and curiosity. Gather some squeeze toys, some crinkly wrapping paper, and a piece of a waxed-paper bag for demonstration purposes. Let him/her try out the new tools (with your assistance) to discover the new sounds.

Three Months Old

Phone-Time: Locate two play phones and disconnect the sound. A cell phone might not be a good idea (broken or not) because he/she might not know the difference. Carry on a two-way conversation (with yourself) for a while, but after your baby notices the changes in tone—you might have some competition for the phone time from that point forward. This exercise is appropriate for babies from three months until around nine months (maybe never).

Dance to the Flashlight: From four months to a year your baby and the kitten might be in competition for the flashlight on the wall/floor trick. All it takes is a darkened room, a grasp on your baby, and a few minutes for some fun.

Four Months Old

Do the Ready—Steady—Up—and Down: Motor and balance issues are now in the picture from about four to seven months. To encourage crawling, place him/her on the tummy and press the palms of your hands against both feet. He/she will recognize the resistance—with time—and be on all fours ready to travel everywhere and more.

Five Months Old

The five-month marker opens the door to the 'Rodeo Ride' event. The game is simply a sense of cause and effect.

1) Sit on the sofa or in a chair with your knees bent (right-angle).
2) Seat the baby facing you on your knees with his/her legs on either side.
3) For extra bounce and support, place your hands around the baby's waist, and gently sing a little about riding the horsey to town. On the final verse, drop the legs apart and let the baby fall (safely) to the floor.

It is up to you for the decision of how many times the pony has to go to town.

Six Months Old

The Shadow Show: Six to fifteen months bring forth your baby's ability to observe shapes and patterns. You can make a show using a flashlight, a blank wall, and your hands. All you need to do is sit on the floor with your baby in your lap.

Hold up your fingers and make some pretend animals. Use your baby's hands to make some shapes. Hand puppets or baby toys can also make some interesting shadows.

Seven Months Old

Hide and Seek: Around the seventh to tenth month; you will notice your baby has acquired some fine motor skills and understanding of object permanence.

Play hide the yummy treat under the cup. Place two pieces of food in front of your baby, and use opaque cups while using another cup with nothing under it. Swirl the cups a bit and see if your youngster can figure out the on without the food.

This is a great tool for a picky eater also. Make his/her life fun and a learning challenge.

Eight Months Old

Diaper Play Time: This game has probably been played with young children for centuries. If your baby has started squirming during the diaper change, he/she has probably gotten bored of the same changing table scenery. Why not play a game of, 'where can we change the diaper?' All it takes is bringing along the essential tools to a new location. Try it sometime.

Nine Months Old

Kitchen Time: It is time for your youngster to learn how to become a chef (with your assistance). It's time to play in your baby's kitchen:

Use a plastic pan and some measuring spoons or cups to play scoop the cereal. Use some colorful round circles or alphabets so he/she can measure all of the ingredients for the new invention for snack time.

Tip: Mom or Dad—you need to supervise so the food doesn't get eaten too quickly and make him/her choke.

Ten Months Old

The Climb Every Cushion Game: The climbing game is a superb game for babies from ten months to eighteen months of age. All it takes is a bunch of pillows, a bit of free space, and some time.

The exercise is a safe way to make a jungle gym in your home. Use some sturdy cushions for the bottom layer, such as bed pillows or couch cushions. For the top of the pyramid use some throw pillows. Try not to make the climb too steep, but he/she will enjoy the new journey with your hand-monitored security.

Eleven Months Old

Your active tyke is probably ready for a bit more action around this time of his/her life. How much more fun can you have than to sing out of tune to the 'Hokey Pokey' tune? That is okay because it is a great way to teach rhythm, musicality, language, and gross motor skills.

Some parents believe letting a child this age use the big bed as a trampoline. The vote is still out on that one. If you open the gate once, you will need to open it again later.

One Year Old

It is birthday time, and what an adventure it has been. Try not to become discouraged along the path. You will get it; it takes practice—you will have plenty of that!

Recommended Toys

A Baby Gym: A newborn can benefit from a baby gym with all of the high contrast objects (especially black and white). He/ she can only see about a foot away. As your baby grows, you can add plastic links/hangers to the design as an additional focal point.

A Set of Plastic Links: The links are great additions for the gym—but don't stop there—hang them from the top of the car seat or stroller. The curves of the link is another texture that must be explored through the hands and mouth. It is a 'win-win' situation; you for organization, and the baby for fun.

Mirror Time: Your child can benefit from this game from infancy throughout his/her year-old birthday. If you have a baby gym, you already have the equipment needed for your youngster to see his/her reflection. If you don't have one; place a full-length mirror where he/she can see how cute the outfit is for today.

Mirrors are great for entertainment, distraction, and motivation. Be sure the mirror is secure and safe to be used around your baby. Special mirrors are available at most baby stores, or online.

Squeezable Bath Toys

"Rubber Ducky" is a great song, but bring on the bag full of instant voices and characters. The hand muscles will surely get a workout just to make the toy squeal. Development skills are encouraged by reaching, grasping, visual tracking, and learning how to bang things together.

Building Blocks: Gone are the days of having no choices of the kind of building blocks your type can use. Now, he/she can play and stack a soft/crinkly block and make some of the greatest sounds (similar to a potato chip bag as it is crinkled). However, the soft texture is a great aid for motivation to move from the tummy and sides into a sitting position. A little incentive (the pretty blocks) can go a long way.

Improvement can be observed as your baby uses eye-hand coordination and the cause and effect (throwing anything, maybe even a temper). Hours and months can be spent on this grand hobby.

Just because you don't have a lot of money in the budget for fancy toys; doesn't mean you cannot make some of your own inventions. After all, many children would rather get into the kitchen cabinet and play with the pan drum instead of playing with the new drum set outside. Go figure. Welcome to the amazing world of children!

Conclusion

Thank you again for downloading your copy of the book; Your Baby's First Year! I hope the information was sufficient to help you to on the process of your baby's development

The next step is to apply everything you have learned during the course of the online adventure. You have heard that babies don't come with instruction manuals. Hopefully, this set of guidelines will make the path a bit easier.

Finally, if you gained some beneficial knowledge, please provide a few minutes of your time to share your thoughts and post a review on Amazon.

Thanks and Enjoy Your Baby!

Description

The information provided should help you with some of the pitfalls you will surely experience with your infant. Everyone (especially you and your baby) should understand everything involved in raising a baby from infancy throughout the first years. Setting guidelines and providing a roadmap is all your bundle of joy needs to start his/her journey.

Reasons to Have This Book as a Guideline for Parenting

> Better Understand Your Baby's First Year
> Physical, Social, & Cognitive Development Steps
> Know What Dad Can Do To Help and Support
> Understand What Your Child Can Eat and What to Avoid
> Recognize and Set Sleeping and Feeding Routine
> Learn How to Breastfeed or Bottle Feed
> Learn How to Bathe Your Baby
> Know What to Do With a Sick Baby
> Know How to Communicate With Your Baby
> Learn Ways of How to Exercise and Play with Your Baby

Learning how to take care of your infant in the first year will help you continue with development for your child for many years to come.

Happy Parenting!

Preview Of - Pregnancy: Your Baby Guide Week For Week

This book gives you a comprehensive understanding of how your baby is developing week for week as well as what it is you should do to ensure you have a healthy and successful pregnancy.

Are you planning to get pregnant, just missed your periods and are suspecting that you could be pregnant or have already confirmed that you are pregnant? If either of these is true, congratulations-you are about to become a mother.

But while this is definitely good news, you probably are worried; worried about whether you will carry the baby to full term, worried about the morning sickness, worried about the health of the baby that you are carrying and such. So what is it you can do to minimize your level of worry? Simple; you equip yourself with as much knowledge about pregnancy as possible so that you can approach it with all the confidence you need.

This book provides all that i.e. knowledge to take you throughout your pregnancy from the 1st week to the day you get to hold your bundle of joy in your arms. It breaks down your term into weeks so you can learn how your baby is developing, how to take care of it while in the womb, the changes taking place in your body throughout the pregnancy and such.

After reading the book, you can bet that you will be better equipped to deal with anything that comes up during the pregnancy from a point of knowledge as opposed to a point of fear. While your doctor/OB may give you much of the information, having lots of knowledge about pregnancy will provide a good enough foundation for your discussions with your OB or doctor even if you are a first time mom.

Pick up your copy today!

Enjoying Reading My Books? Maybe You Want To Read These Books Too

Below you'll find some of my other books that are on Amazon and Kindle as well. Simply click on the links below to check them out.

Want to know when next book is published? Subsribe here: lacobiz.com/kindle-book-club

Pregnancy: Your Baby Guide Week For Week

Pregnancy: Expecting A Baby For New Moms

Parenting: 2-in-1 Box Set Pregnancy Books

Recommended:

Ketogenic Diet: Top 50 Breakfast Recipes

Ketogenic Diet: Top 50 Lunch Recipes

Yoga: Beginners Guide - For Yoga Poses - Easy Steps And Pictures

Mindfulness - Meditation For Beginners – Stress Free Body, Depression And Anxiety Relief

5 Weeks Ketogenic Plan, Weight Loss Recipes - Easy Steps For beginners

Ketogenic: Ketogenic Diet - Mistakes Protection Handbook

Smoothies Cleanse - Detox Diet And Lose Weight In A Healthy Way

Don't forget to subscribe to my newsletter! lacobiz.com/kindle-book-club

Made in the USA
Middletown, DE
11 January 2017